WE WERE ALL
SOMEONE ELSE
YESTERDAY

WE WERE ALL SOMEONE ELSE YESTERDAY

poems

Omar Holmon

—

Published by Button Poetry / Exploding Pinecone Press
Minneapolis, MN 55403 | http://www.buttonpoetry.com

—

Cover design: Kevin Wong

ISBN - 978-1-943735-68-6

24 23 22 21 20   1 2 3 4 5

"You can't win.
Time to start figuring out how not to lose"
—*Valeria Richards (Avengers Vol. 5, #13, 2013)*

Against The World

I'm back home from college
visiting my mother.
I'm sitting on the couch,
and we are both watching TV

can't recall what,
probably a Lifetime movie.

Not of my choosing—

During a commercial she turns to me and says,
"It's not the same when you're away.

The house is usually vibrant
when you're here. It's so quiet now.

Which is fine, but the silence . . .

the silence is so loud."

I hear that loud
as she looks down at her lap,
then raises her head and says,

"Soooooo . . .

I visited the doctor today."

She proceeds to talk about
being diagnosed with cancer

and makes a quip about
how God never gives you more
than you can handle,
then says,

"but shit, this?!"

What I remember most
was the silence in the living room
all the space it took up,

until Mom made room by saying,

"I'm *not* dying today."

She keeps her word.
Does so tomorrow,
And the day after that
Then the years after that

So much so
that it becomes a running joke in the family.

Now
whenever mom says,

"I won't always be here to do this for you,"

my response is,

"How's that possible?

You're way too stubborn to die."

Contents

Anatomy Of A Prayer

1

I can count the number of times I've prayed
on one hand

2

My best friend asks me,
"Why is it every girl you date wants to find God after
they have sex with you?"

I reply,
"I don't know.
Why is it you tell time by saying,
'It's a quarter to whiskey or half past tequila?'"

3

I believe in Murphy's Law:
"Anything that can go wrong,
will go wrong"

4

My father
is a man of science.
I don't know what he believes in.

I'd sooner question if he's found proof to what color
human God bleeds
than ask him

5

My mother is shotgun subtle
when it comes to bad news,
"I rented Erin Brockovich . . .
Julia Roberts has HUUUGE teeth

By the way the cancer is back.
It's in my liver and spine. . . .
Seriously, her teeth are huge."

She believes in God the way I think that everything will
be okay, but I've been watching her
lose faith in her human,
as the presence of a cane becomes a reminder
that her shotgun subtle is becoming sandcastle,

and, whenever people say she is in their prayers,
I become more of my father's son

trying to configure a formula
for the measurement of prayers,
as if I could calculate how many more it will be
until she is allowed to take sitting up
for granted again.

How many more till I believe everything will be okay

6

I ask her if she is afraid
She says no

I ask her if she thinks this is it
She doesn't know.

Then I ask, "Soooo, between you and me . . .
Do you want my brother to be the one to pull the plug
because he is the least favorite?
Cause I figure, if it's gotta be one of the kids to do it . . .
it might as well be *that one*".

She laughs,
says my humor always came like a prayer being
answered for her.

7

All along laughter
has been the anatomy of my prayer.

8

My mother
is too stubborn to die.
Her pride is a Scientific Law that states:
"The will to live is not privilege or birthright; it is fight"

In other words,
"I've had two ex-husbands;
if I can survive their bullshit then I can handle this"

I'm running out of life, not running out of fight.

9

Welcome to the rematch three years in the making
introducing the challenger
with a record of 5.8 million knockouts
due to cancer alone.

The white light at the end of the tunnel!

And our champion,
weighing in at
"none of your damn business,"

sporting a record of 15,000 ass whoopings
over a span of three kids

Isabelle "I'll give you something to cry about" Holmon

10

I believe in Murphy's Law,
"Everything that can go wrong
will go wrong."

But I also believe in anomalies,
that everything that can go wrong

will get better.

I believe

the color human that God bleeds is compassion;

and I believe

the will to live is not privilege or birthright.

It is fight,
it is instinct,

Mom, I still believe
that everything

will be okay.

Such Is Genetics

Every so often mom stops what she's doing,
takes a look at me and says,

"You look like your daddy,"

in a manner that's playful but with a hint of hurt,
as if acknowledging an unspoken betrayal of terms
I was never privy to.

It's like we're on opposite sides of a two-way mirror.
I see a reflection of my own
in her face staring back at me,

but she's on the other side
staring at me and seeing my father.

She'll either
scrunch her face while pursing her lips in a
"Ain't this some shit?" manner,

or

reflect back to when I was a baby,
and remind me yet again of my first word
while thinking aloud,

"You know,
you give them life.
You bring them into this world.

Feed'em. Watch over them.
Bath'em. Burp'em.

And what's the first word out their mouth?!

'Daddy.'"

Then, like a broken clock
about to be right for the second time in the day,

Mom sighs her signature sigh,
shakes her head,

and says,
in a playfully defeated manner,

"Such is life."

I'll Admit It; I Kind of Jumped The Gun On That One

"In Track and Field
there is a rule regarding all sprint races
that if the athlete moves within 0.1 seconds
after the gun has fired, the athlete has false-started"
—Wikipedia

I am 8 years old,
Dad is walking me to a friend's house,
I tell him,

"I don't need you to do this for me."

Looking back
It must be hurtful to hear
such a verbal confirmation that
I'm more my mother's son

Dad asks,
"If someone came after you?
What would you do?"

"I'd run."

He then points to the park two blocks away,
"If you can beat me to that tree
in the middle of the park
Then you're old enough to walk by

yourself."

I accept the challenge.
I mean, I almost tagged Patrick in tag last week,
and he's the fastest kid in school,

I got this.

Dad said "Go" and no lies,
you woulda been proud of me, y'all
I was fucking gone.

I'm up the first block already.
Ain't even goin' look back.
I know I'm good.

It isn't until I get to the second block
that I hear a something in the distance
It sounds like thunder but there's no clouds

I realize it's not coming from above
but from behind me.

I turn around, see my father,
and feel the fear of God being put in me
realizing this is the first time
I've ever seen this man run before.

His form was
1936 Jesse Owens Summer Olympics perfect
Mind you, at 8 years old,
I have no idea who Jesse Owens is
But I somehow now know having seen this man
Barry Allen toward me

I don't know why, but I'm thinking I still got a chance.
I can see the tree; I have to be at least half way.
As soon as I turn my head forward again,

I feel the ground shake,
I look to my left,
Dad was already beside me
He ain't even breathing heavy.

You'd think the worst part of this story
is that my father doesn't even acknowledge me
as he passes me by
but it isn't.

The worst part is
that all I see now is him in front of me,
in a hot salmon pink colored button up
blowing in the wind,

beige shorts,
high socks,
and flip-flops

This man smoked me in flip-flops (fucking flip-flops).

When I finally make it to the tree,
he doesn't smile or say anything.
Just walks beside me as if nothing happened

And for the rest of the way,

I'm hoping
that he doesn't tell mom about this.

My Father Might Be Top 5 Rappers Dead Or Alive

Scene:
My father drives me back home
after spending the weekend with him.
I take the moment to try and connect with him.

I ask, "Why is it after 21 years,
you never said, 'I love you' or
'I'm proud of you'to me?"

My father, eyes never leaving the road, responds,
"Life ain't a TV special."

Scene: I'm in my kitchen with my father,
venting about my significant other.
When I ask for his advice,
he says,

"I . . . don't think I need to know about this.
I just came over to make sure
your taxes are in order."

Scene: I'm in Mom's living room
playing video games with my friend Phil after school.
My father has me pause the game

then tells Phil
to read a passage from the Quran
that he's pointing to.

Phil reads aloud,
"We created man from sounding clay
of altered Black smooth mud."

Dad closes the book,
smiles at us, two black boys,
before saying, "Smoooth Black mud."
and just walks away.

Scene:
I pick up my phone and see a text message
from my father that reads,

"I'm near the land of your youth
looking at an ugly car."

Scene:
In my father's living room,
I state the name of a foreign president
I have just been made aware of.
My father had already known of him
as well as his predecessors.

I ask,
"Why do you know the presidents
of so many other countries?"

He says,

"Americans think it's only important to know their own.
It's important to know others."

Scene: In my sister's living room,
my father meets my partner at the time
for the first time.

We're discussing colonization
and the redistribution of land.

It reminds my father of something
historian John Henrik Clarke once said
in a lecture about colonizers
trying to take land from Africa:

"If you love Africa so much,
we'll give you a piece of it
that you can keep forever.

The length of your body
from head to toe,
6 feet in the ground."

Upside-Down Pineapple Cake

Kece, ever the elder sister,
played matriarch on my 15th birthday
when our mother was in the hospital.

She rose to the occasion
and tried to make a different kind of birthday cake,
an upside-down pineapple cake.

When the yeast didn't follow her lead,
I assured her, "It doesn't matter.
I'll eat whatever you make"

She loves this part of the story.

My favorite part of this story is what happened
a year later on my 16th birthday
when mom walked out the kitchen
carrying an upside-down pineapple cake

saying, "Oh, I just gave it a shot"
in her modest southern,
"What? This ol' thing" manner.

The cake was symmetrically perfect—
Individual pineapples rings baked into golden halos
surrounded by feathers of brown sugar.

She even used the pineapple juice in the batter.
What? Pineapple juice in the batter?! Who does that?
We weren't about to eat a cake,
we were about to literally consume art.

And I remember my sister saying,
"Wow, that looks great."
but looking like she wanted to say,

"Really lady? Really?
Youuuuuuuuuuuuuuu bit—"

And I remember my mom saying,
"Yeah I never tried to make this before."
But looking like she was really saying,

"Yeah.
That's right.
First try.

I still run this."

The Illusion Of Better

It's early spring when my sister
came home a week early from Singapore
to surprise Mom with her 8-month-old grandson.

This will be Mom's first time seeing him.

When Kece arrives,
Mom is still at the mall.
I call her and ask when she'll be back,
there's an errand I have to run.

Mom says she's coming back now,
even after I assure her,

"There's no rush, take your time."

I know her.
If I'm saying there's something I have to do,
she'll hurry up because
she doesn't ever want to be a bother.
Hence, why I called.

I look out the window waiting for her car to pull up.
Kece and her husband put Noah on the couch
(with pillows keeping him in place)
in the living room, so he'll be the first thing Mom sees.

I go down stairs and open the door;
Mom apologizes for taking so long (she didn't).
I say no problem and gesture for her
to go ahead of me up the stairs,

ask if she found what she was looking for.
I keep her talking as she gets to the top of the stairs, she
looks at the couch and shouts . . . a weird Mom noise of
surprise that I can't really translate, honestly.
Sounds like a cross between
a "whoa-uhh" and an "ahhh . . .whoa-aaaah?!" I guess?

Mom moves to pick up her grandson;
her back is toward me as she looks around,
I'm guessing looking for her daughter and son-in-law.

When she turns to me, she's crying what I assume are
tears of joy until she asks me,

"Is this real?"

I know now that they are tears of confusion.
Our mother has ~~schizophrenia~~ a chemical imbalance; we
call it that because, if we call it by what it is,
she'll get defensive.

Every so often she'll grow tired of taking her medicine.
Having to take these pills that make you *you*,
but a slightly different version of you.
A version that's just a bit slower
and always a bit more tired . . .

the cost of keeping both feet in reality.

How cruel a thing to not know
when you can trust your own self.

I can't blame her for wanting to get off medication,
but I do, because
we both know how this ends if she does—
the voices coming back, along with
the hospital forms, gowns, visits,

and having to tell her,
"You can't come home yet.
You have to stay here a little longer."

Thankfully, this is not that.

I made sure Mom was in front of me
going up the stairs;
in case she fell back from shock,

I'm there to catch her physically.

Instead I catch her reality.
And assure her

"Yes,
this is real.
You're holding your Grandson."

My Nephew Learns About Race

Noah: Do I have to be American? Can't I just be Singaporean?

Sister: (Explains difference between citizenship and race)

Me: (Leans into his face) Race is a social construct made to hold you down, my g.

5 minutes later

Noah: I wasn't born yet. I was in your tummy.

Sister: That's right.

Me: (Leans into his face to tell him where babies actually come from)

While Helping My Nephew Assemble An Ice Cream Parlor And Construction Site For His Toy City

Everything is all good playing with my nephew as he built his toy city, until he said . . .

Noah: Now let's do the Police Department.

Me: Yeaaaaah, I don't really . . . fuck with the police, sooo—mmmm I'ma have to tap out on this one.

What follows is a series of grunting noises that he's now adopted from me. When this occurred, I have no clue. I'll translate

Noah: Grhmmmmmm. [Help me]

Me: Grhm. [Police been fucking up, my guy. I'm just—]

Nephew: Grhmmmmmmmmmmmmmmmm.
[My negus, I'm 6. You really 'bout to die on this hill with a 6-year-old trying to build an entire toy city?

This what you doin'right now? We can do police reform and dismantle their systemic oppression in the marginalized neighborhoods afterwards, but shit, can you help me out here?

The parts to snap in for this building are hard, and my fingers are fucking tiny, guy. Shit, man!]

Me: . . .

Nephew: . . .

Me: The helicopter pad sticker goes on top the precinct?

Depends On The Height Of The Bridge

When my brother, Travis, found out his daughter
was making prank phone calls,
the car ride back home turned courtroom.

The only defense her defense team
could present to Travis, now staring into the rearview
mirror at her,—as his father had once done to him—was,
"But everyone else was doing it."

My brother unconsciously channels our mother
and speaks the words she uttered, same as her mother
before her,

"If all your friends were jumping off a bridge,
would you jump too?"

I turn to my left and look at Travis.
This is the first time I've seen him play disciplinarian.
The same man that I once saw eat cereal with orange
juice just cause

has ascended into fatherhood,
has become a responsible adult

I know I should say something responsible as well
but what came out from me was

"If all my friends were jumping off a bridge,
I'd definitely jump."

And on cue,
Travis turns to me and says,
"Oh me too.
What other people think is very important to me."

Having THE Talk With My Nephew

I pulled my nephew aside and gave'em a stern talk
when he wasn't following directions.

"What are you doing?

You keep rushing ahead
not thinking about what's in front of you.

You can't run out in the world like that.
I'm not always going to be here to save you,
and I can't protect you if I don't see you.

What if you got stuck over there?
You've only got one life, man.
You have to be more aware of your surroundings.
Do you understand me?

You don't wanna die, right?
That's not what you want, right?

Okay, then get it together
and eat, stomp, or throw balls of yarn
at these fucking shy-guys, man!
Stop running into them!

Hey, you said you wanted my help in
'Yoshi's Woolly World'.

You gotta be calm playing this
or it'll end up like Super Smash Bros. all over again."

"How Am I Supposed To Explain Regular Human Interactions Between Consensual Adults To My Kid?!"

Noah (age 8): They've been together forever.

Me: That's because they are dating each other.

Noah: What is dating?

Inner me: Shit. He cornered me into being a responsible adult.

Me: Well, when a boy and a girl . . . or a girl and a girl . . .or a boy and a boy . . . or just two (or more) people, like one another and spend time together on purpose.

Noah: If it's a boy and a boy or a girl and a girl that means they're gay.

Me: Yeah. Which is normal.

Noah: Yeah. . . .Is my hot dog ready?

Me: Yeah.

Noah: How many girlfriends have you had?

Inner me: Thought I was home free.

Me: How many do YOU have?!

Noah: None.

Me: Alright then. (**Laughing**) I've dated a few.

New Ways To Smile

Things I know about this girl:
she is cuter than a panda bear
deciding which end of a bamboo stick to eat first
and moves like the martyr of a high school dance floor.

The first sacrifice of carefree,
blooming life from hips and hair,

while the best of us fake inanimate cool because we're
still too afraid of our own bodies,
plus,

I think she's single, cause when the DJ said,
"All the single ladies make some noise,"
I specifically remember her . . . making noise.

Now what follows is a list of things
I'm trying to bring myself to tell her:

1

You are scientific proof
that there are still new ways to smile.

2

The YouTube link I sent you
of two otters, asleep, holding hands, drifting with the
water current—it's the way I say you got this nature that
garners you in remarkable.

3

When I'm like,
"why'd they kill Jazz in Transformers?"
and you're like, "I know right?
What even Black robots die at the end of movies too?"

4

Boy Meets World,
season 4 episode 17,
Topanga Lawrence coming
back 300 miles from Pittsburgh
to Corey Matthews in Philadelphia.

5

We all face our monsters differently,
Just because I smile while I do it doesn't make me any
less serious.

6

When my father was still the man he used to be,
he'd drive 177 miles, 3 hours and 27 minutes,
to see my mother every weekend.

My sister found her husband 3,302 miles away
in Singapore while living in Tokyo;
that's a 55-hour drive through the Pacific Ocean floor.

Destiny has a history of making my bloodline
run the distance.

So, even though your window
is 537 miles 8 hours and 21 minutes that way,

I want to stand outside of it—
even though I don't know which one it is—
with a boom box over my head singing,

"Straight up now tell me, do you really want to love me
forever? Oh. Oh. Oh,"

and you'd be all,
"What are you doing it's 2 o' clock in the morning?"
but I'd be like, "What? I can't hear you
over the sound of all this awesome!"

7

Roy Sullivan was a park ranger
that got struck by lightning 7 times

and lived.

The human body is a beautiful conductor,
our words
hydrogen bond.

I held your hand,
felt every electron coursing the current
on the life line in your palm,

and had a flash forward of us looking back
discussing when we first met
to smaller four-eyed fragments of ourselves.

This is complex simple science,
but you are the most gorgeous social science,
because I've been treating each phone conversation
as research

on what smiles sound like.

New Ways to Smile: Epilogue

"New Ways to Smile"
is the only true love poem I have ever written.
10 years later, I am still not able to top it.

This isn't a poem
about the deeper meaning behind a love poem
or being stuck in a moment on someone;
I'm literally just saying, I am still not capable
of writing a better love poem than that one.

I capped myself. It's got everything—
Otters holding hands, nerd homages,
long distance relationship references,
and the scene from *Say Anything*
with John Cusack holding a boom box over his head.

I literally reenact that scene each time
when saying that line.
Even the woman I was dating at the time,
who's also a writer, said,

"Yeah. You can't top that."

Years later. She jokingly
(but low-key seriously) asked about
when I'd write her a love poem.

Know that if two writers are dating each other,
they both want this
No matter how much they protest,

I mean,
who wouldn't want to see the words
their partner would use for their paged portrait?
Knowing full well they'll find out
once or if they ever break up.

Anyway,
she legit looked me in the windows of my soul
and told me,

"You're capped for love poems right here."

To which I said,

"I know. That's what I'm saying! I mean, you can take
this one if ya want, since I guess it doesn't really apply
anymore."

"What? No, I want my own," she retorted,
I then remembered
that, technically,
I kinda wrote one for her.

"Ehhhh, it's not the same tho.
That's about your mother; I just make a cameo
appearance."

She was not wrong.
I couldn't do anything else but apologize.
Like, yeah . . . that's literally the best I've got;
me from 2009 did way better than I ever could.

According to @Uberfacts on twitter

"Your mind spends about 70% of its time replaying
memories and creating scenarios of perfect moments."

When I recall the memory, we were both young and
always on-again-off-again talking to each other but
today the distance between us would be shortened for a
day bringing us both face to face.

Knowing this, I did some preparation—
Google'd the key signs of attraction that one would be
able to recognize (don't judge me or my Google search
history).

When you were talking,
I remember repeating to myself:

"Women have 52 signals that they use to flirt 12 of
which involve the eyes"—

and checking off each one
that I remember seeing you do—
"but the most important is the triangle gaze

where eye contact is made, then their eyes drop
down to your lips then back
to your eyes.

It's a sign that they want to be kissed."
I notice this 3 times before we both go for it

Everything that follows that moment
doesn't move in real time to me.
It feels, at best, cinematic,

as if it's all scripted—from the swaying of the grass to
the way the rain comes down as if on cue.

We held hands running through it, looking for any type
of canopy salvation we could find. If life is a carbon
copy of art, then this night has to be the climax of my
life's chapter (or so I believe. ~~You told me you were~~
~~dating someone and I knew that no matter the outcome~~
~~of this night once distance and miles reestablishes being~~
~~a factor between us, you both would work it out.~~

It doesn't last.

I can see that clear as anything I've ever believed in; you
couldn't. ~~Knowing~~ that ~~the now of the~~ then ~~would be the~~
~~last amount of time I'd have with you. I just wanted to~~
~~be in that moment a while longer. However, guilt was~~
~~calling you to leave, and~~ you said I had to let you go . . .

So I did.

~~The next day you called to tell me that you both decided~~
~~to try and work it out.~~

And you said, I had to let you go.
So I did.
And I've been ~~regretting it to myself~~

~~Lying to myself~~

~~reminding myself~~

telling myself,

    I have ever since.

"Continue?"

Mom's favorite video game is Street Fighter II.

We played it when it first came out.
I had to wait a week to play it,
cause I was grounded.

That remains the longest week of my life.

Mom even used to read me
the instruction manual for the game as a bedtime story.
That's how hard we rode for Ryu and the crew.

Remember Street Fighter II's
"Do you wish to continue?" screen?
It appeared after you got lost
or got your shit rocked,
depending upon how good you were.

I think that was Mom's favorite part of the game.

She'd always press continue;
no matter what, she'd keep going on.

Mom is a fun type of competitive.
She'd let my sister win at cards
till she got too good to let that keep goin on.

One time,
I came home from competing in a poetry slam;
Mom was on the couch in the living room.

Mom: You lost.
Me: How'd you know?
Mom: (smiles) Because when you win, you make noise
coming up the stairs, no matter what time it is.
But when you lose,
you come in quiet, like a church mouse.

Me: Ha. I didn't win, but I made the team.
Mom: That's good. I just . . . mmmm
(motions championship belt around her waist)
I just wanted one more.

A few days later,
we saw a commercial for Street Fighter IV on TV.
Mom got so excited, asking,

"Do you have the console for that?
Can we get the game?"

Funny. Years later,
and she still wanted to
continue the game.

Then,
years later,
she wasn't able to press continue anymore.

On The Good Days

My mother died on September 9th, 2011.
For eight years, it's been the same day every day.
On the good days, I'm beside her hospital bed again.

Her breathing is a prizefighter
refusing to throw in the towel.
In the moment, I'm sure she's fighting for her life
Looking back, I think she was fighting against letting it
go in front of me.

But this is a good day.

So hindsight doesn't argue over semantics.
I'm allowed the memory of being her youngest child,
reminding her that her eldest daughter and son are on
their way.

Each breath,
a balled-up fist being thrown on instinct
Slow and wide, but still thrown,
and that's all that matters

when you're over your allotted time.

But I did say this is a good day,

where I remember
one of our last conversations

I lean over and say,

"Mom. If you want to tell me who the favorite kid is, now is probably the best time. I'm just saying"

Mom says,

"You're. . . .

All . . . . .

My

Favorite."

For Those Who Need Both Hands To Lift Mjölnir

My father's basement
is a graveyard to everything I was.

I'll say it plainly.

Everything in Dad's basement is filled
with my share of Mom's memories
I can't decide if all the artifacts
make up a treasure chest or a mausoleum.

Regardless, Tasha and I archeology through
the pieces that made up my whole
before they became parts of a hole.

I'll say it plainly.

I kept holding on to all these pieces of Mom.
Now it's time to see what keepsakes I'll keep,
cause I keep everything well kempt inside

but, physically, I can't keep everything unkept,
as everything I've kept bottled isn't keeping
well.

The irony is lost on me that I'm dishing this
out of me as I'm unboxing dishes, until
I spot a jewel at bottom of the box.

This forgotten relic of my mother,
thawed out of time.

Her cast-iron skillet.

Tasha is Australian-Indian.
Meaning, our culture gap is two oceans thick.

I explain how
"a cast-iron skillet
is the staple of every Black household.
Sometimes you don't even know
how there's one in the house.

It just appears one day and you accept it."

Instantly, I remember Mom cooking,
lifting the skillet from the stove with one hand,
while I need two just to hold it—

wonder if my negligence made it heavier
as the rust has spread thick as the cancer
that took its previous chef's life

but Tasha believes the relic still salvageable.

When we get home,
she turns my sister's kitchen counter
into an operating table.

Lady Macbeths the spots of corrosion with steel wool
before baptizing the skillet in the sink.

Every time she pulls it up from the water,
she inspects it as if looking for a pulse of a memory,

while my sister and I watch from the doorway,
both too afraid of what this resurrection
may unbox from us

but Tasha—
Tasha can't let dead things lie.
For two nights in row,

she oils the pan and heats it in the oven.

On the third night,
she calls me into the kitchen saying,

"It's done."

She hands the skillet over while smiling
before telling me,

"I hope you know this is mine now."

And I'm about to argue that
this iron is my birthright

but I don't,

because I see how many hands she needs to lift it.

Gallows Humor

"All the honors go to the tragedy for chewing up the scene, while the comedian, who has to be much more subtle to be funny, is just loudly criticized when he doesn't come through"—Edmund Gwenn

Funny thing about death:
just before his own, Edmund Gwenn said,

"Dying is easy, comedy is hard."

Funny thing about dying:
Hours before my mother became past tense,

she said,

"When I go . . . Don't bring me back,"

and I replied,

"Given the weight of the current situation,
that's probably the most gangsta shit
you ever said to me."

Funny thing about her last words:
She made a joke right before saying them,

and I wasn't there to hear it

Eventually Somebody Has To Be The Last Of Us

On a night
that was like any other night,
Dad calls me.

We're discussing something,
then talking about the amount of money
I managed to put in my savings account.

If I didn't know any better,
I'd say he's proud of me.
Perhaps for him,
47 years past the age most Black folk don't get to see,

this is what he wanted to see.

When Dad turned 65,
I asked how he was going to spend his birthday.

"I had planned to continue spreading
the 15 cubic yards of topsoil I bought, but
I may just take a nap."

Wonder if the American dream
looked like this for everyone, or perhaps
just Black folk that lived long enough to seize it.

Anyway,
he's still stuck on how much I was able to save.
I let him know,
"I've done things way harder than this."
"Still," he says,

"It's impressive, most impressive.
If my friends were around,
I'd talk to them about you for 10,000 hours."

I don't know what to say to that.
I forget that my father's been surrounded by ghosts
longer than I.

He's the last of his friends.
Friends he knew since kindergarten,
friends his teachers would confuse him for.

He's the last one left.

I don't know that type of alone.

Not yet.

El Dorado Is A Taste, Not A Place

"Insanity is doing the same thing over and over again
expecting different results."—Rita Mae Brown

For seven years,
I've been perfecting insanity
toward a recipe my mother left behind for
a macaroni and cheese roux.

Her version isn't written down
But she showed mc once,
a quarter of my lifetime ago.

The only way to retrace her steps
is to become sixteen again.
Standing in our kitchen,

stirring the cheese roux,
then watching her, chef-careful,
pour portions of the sun over the macaroni.

After a half hour, as if guiding a sword back home from
a foreign body,

Mom would unsheathe her dish out the oven
revealing a road of breadcrumbs
cast in an El Dorado Brown coating.

Yet, in the now,
whenever I attempt a way back to that road
sigh the coordinates aren't right.
The trail doesn't look the same,
which means it won't taste the same.

Despite this, my siblings say,
"Omar, this is good."

                                    "Lies!"
Then their children,
with the bounce of cheerful echo chime in
"I like it Uncle Omar."

                                    "More lies!"

On the eighth year
Tasha, my partner,
charts the path with me.

When we sheathed the mac and cheese
into the oven as if guiding a sword into a foreign body
I thought to myself:

"This is a final boss battle I keep losing"
but what happens if I win?

What does it mean to win?
If I get it right this time it still won't bring her back
So what's the point?

Mom made a point of saying,
"I won't always be around to do this for you,"
and it's hard when the one who use to do this
is no longer here to do it.

After a half hour, we take out the dish
I see the same road I did at sixteen,
It looked the same, and like I knew it would

it tasted the same.

It takes the two of us together
to make the same dish
Mom did

alone.

I've done this for years

alone.

But I get it right
with Tasha

and I always thought
that when I'd finally gotten it right

that maybe

it would make accepting
that she's gone
easier.

It didn't.

She was still
gone

and, like I knew it would,

nothing changes.

A Case Study In Black Girl Magic

After being dumped on New Year's Day,
which is two weeks before my birthday,
I'm in my room processing this and pouting (keyword:
pouting)

when my mother walks by, opens the door, and says,
"If you're going to cry over a girl . . .
at least cry over one with her own hair" (*Slams door*)
to which I reply

"I'm not crying, you're crying. Shut up."

I believed what we had was magic
until Mom teaches me to spot the sleight of hand.

Magic is defined as an extraordinary power,
seemingly from a supernatural source.

I watch a girl made of California love
unwrap strands from silk scarf cocoon that
blooms curl-shaped petals,

waters each with her own concoction made from
lemon juice, coconut oil, avocado, and shea butter.
I feel like I'm watching an alchemist
turn wool into Golden Fleece.

I ask,
"Does this ritual ever make you feel like a wizard?"
She says,

"Muggles wouldn't understand this magic."

I see no illusion in her art.
The closest I've come
to understanding Black girl magic
is in the story of Henrietta Lacks,

a Black woman
who had cells from her cervical cancer . . .
"unknowingly" donated to science.

It was discovered her cells can be kept alive indefinitely.

Now a Black woman living after her death,
becoming the blueprint for cures after her death,
what could be more Black girl magic than that?
What could be more supernatural source than that?

They have become known as

"the immortal cell line."
her name, race,
and family aren't afforded the same luxury.
Notice when in the name of science,

history will say "donated,"
when they mean taken;
history will say "cultivated,"
when they mean stolen;
history will say "discovered,"

when they mean,
"Look at what we own now."

By all rights this should mean
that Black girls can be defined as
a supernatural source
from which extraordinary power
is constantly being derived.

I know this to be no sleight of hand,
when moments after my mother has become past tense,
I sit with my head on her deathbed,
apologizing for not being there.

"I'm sorry" became
my mantra,
my incantation,
my last ingredient to a spell
I want to believe would bring her back
if I just mean it enough.

Years later,
I meet a girl made of sea salt and tonic
and the things they say about her,

heard she a slave ship's reckoning,
says her path to America was an immortal line
of outstretched Black hands from the Atlantic.

I see the lord's work when she walks,
hear an unorthodox book of memory in her laugh,
taste the remnants of a spell
she casts in a cauldron of Black lipstick

as I bestow the biggest honor I can think of and say,
"My mother would have loved you."

Because my mother is . . .

Because my mother was . . .
Magic.

Prelude: So We Hear This Commercial About A Toaster

Two to three times a week,
I drive my mother from Lodi, New Jersey,
to get chemotherapy
at Sloan and Kettering
in New York.

It's a trip neither of us want to take.
Her, because she doesn't want to have cancer
(obviously).
Me, because
I don't want my mother to have cancer (also obvious)
and driving in New York is like Mario Kart.

We do what we must, regardless.

On one trip, we hear a commercial for a toaster
from a company
called Burnt Impressions.
Not just any toaster, a toaster
that sears the image of Jesus onto slices of bread.

I can't tell you anything else
that advertisement said,
but for the rest of the drive
we laugh at that commercial.

We were still laughing at it
while Mom was gets her chemo done.

I take out my laptop,
sit beside her chair,
and start writing a poem
about this Jesus toaster,

showing each line for her to make sure
I'm not being hella blasphemous.

We've never done this before.

Usually, when she's going through her chemotherapy,

she'll tell stories of my sister and brother
where I was too young to remember.

When she gets to me being born
(let's be honest, the best part)
and our time together up until now,

she always stops for a moment,
looks at me, then says,

"It has always been the two of us;
It's always been us against the world."

Jesus Christ Super Toaster

During a phone conversation over religion,
I told my ex that I didn't pray.
I believe in God, but it's just something I don't do.

After this discovery, she said she didn't know if she
could date me anymore,
said I wasn't devout in my faith.
I said, hold on.

How you goin' judge me?
Sayin', "I'm lost?"
Sayin', "I'm not devout in my faith?"
Sayin', "I'm not a man cause I like to sleep with a
sunflower night-light on?"

"I didn't say . . . you told me that was a Glade Plug-in"

"Whatever yo . . . Listen!"

I then proceeded to inform her . . . I'm sorry,
school her, on a small company in Vermont
that produced a toaster that burns the image of Jesus
Christ onto slices of bread.

I don't know what the name of the company is,
so let's just call it freaking awesome,
because 40 dollars later plus shipping and handling . . .
guess who's got a freaking awesome toaster?

That's right, me, and it doesn't even stop there!
This toaster knows no race, gender, or creed,
it accepts all types of bread equally.

I'm talking White bread, Rye Bread,
Pompernickeeeeeel (ha), Raisin bread (ha),
Sour dough (ha).

I even customized it so that when the toast pops up,
the toaster goes,

"Ahwwwwwwwwwww"

and doves fly out.

If that isn't devotion (huh), I don't know what is.
Then I told her, how you goin' judge me
when I seen Devil ham in your pantry?

What? Blasphemous!
Devil Dogs all in your delicatessen!
What? That's straight blasphemous!

Me? I have breakfast with Jesus every day.
Can I get some sour cream?
Now who said they can't believe it's not butter,
(what?!)? You can't believe?
Let the breakfast club say amen!

Now pass the jam!
Said I love me some Jesus.

My Jesus is great (well).
My Jesus is strawberry preserves on whole wheat.
My Jesus is delicious as a mutha fucka
with some cream cheese.

When I die,
my will shall dictate that I be buried with my
Jesus Christ Super Toaster (I don't know what the actual
name of the toaster is, so I call it that),

and when I roll into heaven on a fire-breathing yellow
hippopotamus, iPod in one hand and Jesus Christ Super
Toaster in the other,

Jesus is going be all, "What up Omar?"
I'll be like "Nothing."
He'll say, "That's cool."

Then I'll say, "Here, this is for you, Jesús,"
and he'll be like, "whaaaaaaaaaaaat!!?"
And when that first piece of toasty delicious pops up in
front of him, making him think
he's looking in a stained glass breaded mirror,

Jesus'll be like, "Oh my Gawd this shit is hot son."
Now I know what you're thinking, and yes,
this is what Jesus sounds like in my head
and on Facetime.

He'll be all happy, saying,
"That's me yo! Yo, Dad check this out.
Where Lucifer at? I'ma rub it in his face
like ahhhhh stings don't it. Take that. Take that."

Now mind you
she actually hung up somewhere around
Jesus being delicious with some cream cheese,
but I kept going on anyhow cause, the way I see it,

if heaven has a sense of humor,
I'm so in there,
and if it doesn't, well,

I had a good run.

Occelus

The eyes on a peacock's tail feather
are called an Occelus

I know that peacocks
have a huge need for companionship
alone they get heartbroken

I am alone now
I doubt I am a peacock,
I mean

I doubt that I am a heart broken

Nominee For Best Picture Of The Year

The documentary of our
What almost was
got nominated for best picture of the year
for the way it broke the conventional,

"You wanna grab a cup of coffee sometime?"

of romantic comedies.

I wanted to congratulate you
on your nomination
for best lead actress in the role of girl
that smells of shorelines and Sunday mornings.

I'm sure we can agree
God will win for best director. . . . again.

You should know,
there isn't another actress that could make my blood
run clumsy like you.

Your suggestion
that my palms should cup your face like oasis water
during our kissing scene was movie-magic subtle.

The rain came background-music-slow.

The following scene
was the most honest monologue I've ever performed.
I went off script and told you

that you made everything make sense,
and after I confessed
the most honest I'd ever known,
the close-up that captured
the brown girl of your cheeks
blushing sunrise in full bloom
didn't soften your delivery in the line

where you told me
that the fifteen minutes of fame into my finest hour

was on another man's time.

Did you know that fruit flies have a gene
named after the Tin Man from the Wizard of Oz?
If the gene isn't present, the flies do not develop a heart.

I have been trying to act like rumors of my heart
have been greatly exaggerated,
but maybe this is the point in the movie

where

it stops being about the girl

and more about the man

I thought I was supposed to be.

The Heart Is A Play In Two Parts

Part I

I can't help but believe that
if the women I loved were gathered at a table

the general consensus among them would be

"Okay . . . The good thing about Omar is that he doesn't
take anything seriously . . .
The bad thing about Omar is that he doesn't take
anything seriously . . .

The sex was amazing tho . . .

Make sure you write that part down."

Part II

My love is gentrification at its best—
once it's over, I bury every recollection of familiar
under high rises and parking lots

till my heart doesn't recognize the neighborhood,
can't afford the cost of living,
and is forced out of where he grew up,

all the while complaining
that he still has the right to be here

as if he had some say in the matter,
as if he thinks I won't burn this bridge between us
just because I'm still standing on it.

All of which is to say—

Do you know how long it took to be

"okay"

with "not being okay"?

You call that heartbreak?

There are a number of times
where the living room turns into a confessional,
with Mom playing the part of active listener,
asking what's the matter while doing some chore.

On this occasion, it is a matter of the heart.

She's doing the dishes
while I tell her about a girl a few states over,

how luck placed someone else in front of her, before,—
why am I dragging this out?
I'm telling her about the girl from the poem on page 59,
"Nominee for best picture of the year."

I had thought we had the possibility of something before
finding out she had a boyfriend.
And I *knew* they would work things out.

I stare at the floor,
and mom walks out of the kitchen,
drying off a dish. She doesn't look up from the
porcelain, and I figure, when she does,

I'll get the sitcom-mom response of,
"There's other fish in the sea," or, "Well her loss."
Once the dish is dried to her standards,

Mom looks at me
slumped over on the couch and says,

"Good."

Didn't see that coming at all.
I look back at her, confused, and say,

"What?"

Mom responds again,

"Good. She's not leading you on.
She told you what it is.
I mean things happen, sure.

At least y'all had that moment.
Nothing you can do about it.

Good on her."

After two marriages,
two divorces, and three children,

Infatuation isn't stable enough ground
for me to posture against what she's said.

Copper

I'm sitting across from all of her vast.
Now, when I say vast

I'm talking ocean
I'm talkin' this table between us
been keeping me afloat.

She got natural that looks like a wildfire
Caught in the heat of the moment.

Looks like my mother's favorite love song on vinyl
skippin' in a loop of curls and shea butter
and she talks pretty
talks so pretty

says

"We'd have cute brown babies."

So much so that it makes me
want to home equity loan with her

Get the milk after work for her
make SUV soccer mom of her

knowing the children
would be an uncanny shade of copper.

Yet we're still in an age where people believe
such a skin color means they're already dressed for a
funeral.

Where 17 is the new 21 we pray they get to cross.

Pray they get to school, store, mall, movie, date,
love, hurt, heal, live, live, live, live, live.

Every day is a prayer for them to live
but above all things

pray that they come back.

Before someone discovers the worth
in the weight of their copper,

because the world takes.

Before the night hollows the pretty from their talk,

because the world takes.

Pray.

That the wildfire of their hair

stays lit.

The 4C Complex

"The hedgehog's dilemma is a metaphor about the challenges of human intimacy. It describes a situation in which a group of hedgehogs seek to move close to one another to share heat during cold weather. They must remain apart, however, as they cannot avoid hurting one another with their sharp spines. Though they all share the intention of a close reciprocal relationship, this may not occur, for reasons they cannot avoid."—Wikipedia

The Black girl dilemma, or sometimes "The type 3a through 4c kinky hair" dilemma, is an example about the challenges of white folks touching a Black woman's hair without permission. It describes a situation in which a group of Caucasians / strangers seek to satisfy their curiosity about said Black girl without awareness or consideration for said Black girl's feelings, existence, or well-being.

Though the Caucasian will perform a dance of words to say their intentions are "well meaning", they cannot avoid the inevitable offending of the Black girl. Though they "mean well," making contact with a Black girl's hair, however, will not occur, for reasons they both cannot avoid.

Now, there's no term to explain the occurrence of when a Black girl and a Black boy explore one another's hair, but I came close to defining it, in a bar, in Brooklyn, when I had been Black boy sitting with Black girl. The both of us attempting to water-to-wine ourselves from strangers to friends, and what better way then the decision to navigate her fingers through the soft of my forest. Notice her mouth reveal a crescent moon when she sees her fingers disappear into my midnight.

I raise my hand, stop, then ask,
"May I touch your hair?"

She replies,
"Yes, you may."

I feel there's something more to be said
when a Black woman gives you permission
to touch ~~her hair art~~ God.

And how do you describe this texture of God?
This chorus of coarse?
A thick quilted hymn?

When a Black woman gives you permission
to touch her hair, it's a front row seat to so much sky.

A crown of clouds that look
like a succulent,
no, a weeping willow,
or maybe a heart-shaped to bloom in full?

I don't have the words,
just a calm of trust
running my fingers around the summit of her hair.
For us, we're exploring each other's altars.

But I imagine to onlookers,
the both of us,
hair thick as quills,
must look like two hedgehogs

admiring each other's spines.

Ever Wonder What Happens When Someone Says "All Lives Matter" Five Times Into A Mirror

"Said it before and I'll say it now:
America is really fortunate that Black people only want
equality and not revenge."—Joel D Anderson

We say Black lives matter
they critique how we mourn

We say, Black lives matter
they talk politics at the wake

and then
have the savior of a solution
to say

"All lives matter . . ."

They say all lives matter
and America's fruits turn a strange sour

They say all lives matter
and reparations crash Wall Street to collect

They said all lives matter
and thousands of Black bodies

came marching out of the Atlantic.

A Spade Stay A Spade

"Lets call a spade a spade, not a gardening tool"

Refers to calling something as it is
Speaking bluntly without "beating around the bush"

For example,

A Black boy: one strike
A Queer Black man: two strikes
A Queer Black woman: three strikes

An unarmed Black man: threat
An unarmed Black woman: disposable
An unarmed Black child: armed and dangerous

A well-dressed Black woman: unsafe
A well-spoken Black man: not safe
A well-mannered Black child: Still not safe

An Angry Black man: unjustified
An Angry Black woman: unstable
An Angry Black child: unruly

A Black girl: too much
A Black woman: not enough
A Trans Black woman: less

A Black person: the set-up in a joke
A Black culture: the delivery of a joke
A Black life: a punch line that's never not funny.

Niggas In Middle-Earth

*"At an open casting call for background hobbits in the
movie The Hobbit, an Indian woman showed up and was
told, 'No, You can't be in this movie, because you're too
brown to be a Hobbit'"—Wyatt Cenac*

Meanwhile in Middle-Earth
me and my niggas tying bandanas
around the horns of our unicorns

There's a horde of macro-aggressions
headed towards us
and we ready to ride out

cause I'll be God damned
if they gentrify our homeland

that +999 pantom armor on my chest
dripping candy paint got this shit looking like
Black death excellence

got this shit lookin like,
"what dragon goin' smite me?"
I'm thinking, no white privilege conjured against me
shall prosper

but if it does, they'll have to roll the die
with the steel piece on my side
an obsidian blade on my hip called "Perfect Dark"

given to me by the Lady Yonce of the lake.
She said, "It's dangerous to go

and be Black boy alone, take this . . ."
right before she Black Girl Magic'd
a sword of peak Blackness onto the kid
when it leaves the sheath
all you hear is, "Awwww, shit",
with each swing in battle,
you can hear it sing the names of all my lost kin,

sounds like thousands of Black bodies
calling for the blood of whatever false God
these sorcerers of love and light scapegoat
their actions behind

whatever false God deemed "white magic"
the privilege to the rite of being right

Just so you guys know
this totally isn't a race war metaphor
happening or anything . . .

The readers of this should know
this is totally a metaphor for the race wars . . . that is in
fact coming

And I roll with a squad of South Side Sages
that rock their wizard hats cocked to the side like fiddy
caps

elder scrolls taped across their waist
spells tat'd across on they neck
down for a fly by, ridin' on a Griffin
with that Rosewood wood wand

locked and loaded
with a banana clip of mana in the chamber,
shoutin,

SOUTH SIDE, Hufflepuff till I die.
We products of our environment
none of us sure if we'll live to see twenty one
thousand years of age
I buried a brother-in-arms last night

her body

a pine box wrapped gift back to the Earth,
her spear
still chest deep through a Cyclops that bit off
more than he could fuck with

but that won't make the front page
of your local fiction novel

cause they wanna say
we don't belong here
as if we didn't exist in this time,
as if we ain't from the same Middle Earth

When my mother's mother fought
Direwolves, Giants, and Kings
drunk off their own manifest destinies
to keep this piece of Earth in her family for 5 millennia

so I'll be damned if we give home up

be damned if our banner comes down
be damned if I come back on my shield
without a fistful of crowns to show that we here
That we'll always be here

on our piece of Earth
from the same Middle-Earth

drunk off our own divinity

The Blackest Night Of My Life

was a Friday night on Frederick Douglass Boulevard
in Harlem
sitting in a restaurant enjoying the company
of a macaroni and cheese filled skillet
that accompanies my first taste of
catfish and grits
as Tupac's *Ambitionz Az a Ridah* baptizes the room

"In the parties where it be so packed"

The most African-American night of my life
was my first time in
South Africa
standing in a room full of countrymen singing songs of
their nation
word-for-word by heart as I just stood there
listening to my lover sing wither countrymen
I'm here
in the moment
not alone but
alone
ashamed the songs I know adhere to a different flag
American boy
stranger in a land that he should call home
foreigner in a land that's for his own but not his own

"Where that atmosphere be so black"

Colonization

She asks about my day
I tell her how a mosquito broke in while I was working,
made itself an intruder before I made it a mural on the
wall

She questions why I decided to kill it

I answer

She asks,

"Have you heard Aziza Barnes' poem about killing a
centipede?"

"I thought a colonizer's thought not "I'm sorry"
or   "I shouldn't have killed it" but "if I don't kill it
now, how   will I find it again?"

Her accent has this air of royalty that always escorts the
point she's making

I stare at her matter-a-factly,

then lovingly

Later that night,

after our mouths have said all they could
and our bodies speak for themselves,

I head towards the kitchen, turn on a light,
and see that a roach has infiltrated our Airbnb

I hear the royalty of her accent turn an uncivil sour
as she call me by my surname and shouts,

"kill it!"

Timberland boot in hand,
I'm about to rain down the queen's justice upon the
intruder,

Then, mid-swing, I stop,

stare at her lovingly,

then matter-a-factly, as I ask,

"But isn't this the colonizer's thought?"

To which she replies

"No! That roach *is* the colonizer
and it must be stopped!"

10 Things I Want To Say to a Black Nerd

After Jenifer Falu's
"10 Things I want to say to a Black Man"

1
It's so hard being a Black nerd

2
The books you love
don't have many heroes or villains that look like you
It's not the color but the content of
the characters that keep you reading

3
You thank God for Donald Glover
and his songs as Childish Gambino
Listening to him is the like having Nikola Tesla sitting
shotgun in The Delorean

while doing Pi . . .sorry, "donuts" in a Game Stop
parking lot, top down as Tesla says,
"Is that the new Afrofuturism mixtape?
Homie, TURN. THAT. SHIT. UP!"

4
Batman's superpower
is generational wealth and stock options.
That has nothing to do with the rest of the poem,
I just felt it really needed to be said

5
There is nothing more beautiful than a Black nerd girl
Any time you hear'em rep their fandoms,
you Dance Dance Revolutions round your heart

If she has natural hair
and wants to converse about Converse?

+10 damage points
Talks trash whenever she beats you in Mario Kart?
+25 skill points

If she watches Craig of Creek
and writes her own fan fiction,
there's, no calculation for how sexy that is

6
When you get the girl,
you'll remember every detail,
like how the paint on her nails
chips into isolated islands

When you get the boy, you'll reminisce
on how he made oblivious look like the new abstinence

When you have each other,
you'll recall the memory as an 8-bit adventure;

call it old-school, call it classic,
whatever symbolizes
that the moment was an arcade high score
you both achieved together

7

Your most hood moment on Game of Thrones
when they killed Ned Stark
Even as I mention it now,
inside you're saying to yourself,

"They killed my niggga Ned Man"
They killed my nigga Ne—!"
For nerds, Ned Stark's death is equivalent to
when Hip-Hop heads lost Biggie Smalls
or when Friends went off the air for white people

8

Your black friends say
hand over your black card
because you never watched "The Wire"

Your white friends think,
having watched "The Wire,"
it's okay for them to say

they're "blacker" than you are

since nerd is the new Black,
so, "Everybody wanna be a nerd
but don't nobody wanna be a nerd"

9

A nerd-off is the closest you will ever come
to battle rap
It occurs whenever someone
corrects you on a topic obnoxiously

If you engage in this Battle Royale of facts,
your retort should always sound something like this:
"Actually, Blade is the movie that kick-started all these
other superhero movies . . ."

and once you see that look of
"Oh they bout murder me" on their face,

you Highlander them with a stare thats says,
"You goin get this work,

cause I'm a Grayskull graduate
with a Masters in the Universe
and you ain't bout this life b"

10
It is so hard being a Black nerd,
slinging six-sided-dice on the block,

keeping it retro
when you pop out the Nintendo 64
like it's a six-fo Impala,

all Black everything
because that's what you've always been . . .

everything.

From
Chuck Taylors to lightsabers

From
"Press Start" to "Game Over"

Pretty Women Love Puns

During brunch
with the woman I love more than my own life
and the siblings she'd protect with all of her own

she has taken a picture of all of us,
herself included, and dubbed it the breakfast club.
Where that would be enough for most,

my love is not most, and an Instagram caption
must be more than enough in order to do the most
For the moment at hand,

she's come up with
punny brunch names for everyone
but is stuck on the coup de grace for her own.

I assess the situation.
She's wearing purple,

which reminds me that she likes grapes,
which makes me think of John Steinback's book.
I ask if she likes crepes.

Of course she does.

And then it hits me.
I lean back in my chair,
thanking the heaven above for this blessing.

As an
"Oooooooooooooh"
holy spirits its way out of me,

she knows I got something good
"You're gonna wanna marry me for this,"
and she replies,
"I already do. Tell me."

I stare at her face lovingly,
then matter-a-factly.

"Crepes of Wrath"

Her jaw,
a withdrawn drawbridge from amazement

I, knowing full well this is by far
the best pun I'll ever make,

smug as I've ever been,
with arms spread-eagle
ask, repeatedly,

"How much do you love me right now?"

The words rush out her mouth
as a welcoming party of affirmation

as she hits post, turns to me,
shows a pearl throne room smile

and says,

"I'd marry you on the spot."

Pretty Women Love Puns: Epilogue

After a playful (but low-key kinda serious) discussion about taking last names, the woman I love more than my own life says, "Why is it I (women) must give up who I (they've) been for years and take on your (the man's) last name? What of the culture I come from that my children will then never know because my surname is gone?"

Let it be known, she is dropping nothing but straight facts and bars on me. If this was a battle rap, she's killing me right now. All my dumbass got to retort with is not really a damn thing because she is entirely right. I'm just like, "I mean you're super right. I just. Ahhhh—I don't wanna be the only one with this name tho? Ugh, ya wanna hyphen it out?! We gonna surname hyphen compromise?!" (which still has me like boooo and I know I know my patriarchy is showing. I know!) and she says, "Why don't you take my last name then?"

Listen, I go full puppy dog eyes with the quiver voice as I say, "But . . . then I gotta become someone else and" "Exactly!" she smiles as she points out, "Everybody wanna be a feminist but don't nobody wanna be a feminist." Oh, oh, she got me. Whenever she busts that line out against me, I know that she got me and got me good. I'm talking back against the wall, and she knows it. Best I can do is table the conversation by trying to buy time and saying, "Lemme see what my Dad says."

Mind you, she's the whole reason I'm even closer with my father. My mother was the fun parent. The one I'd talk to about everything and she's not here anymore. Instead, it's my dad, the serious parent. After I moved all Mom's stuff out the apartment, my father suggested I come live with him, and when I declined he asked "Why" and I say, "I wanna figure it out myself" and what I don't say is that I'm angry. What I don't say is that she did everything she was supposed to, prayed to her God, did right by everyone, and she isn't here anymore but you are. What I don't say is, "It should have been you."

However, now isn't then anymore. So when your partner loves you enough to tell you about yourself, that you shouldn't push away a parent that is trying (in their own way) just because it's not how you think it should look or be, you listen. So now I answer when Dad calls. Now I ask him what I would have asked Mom. I bring up the surname conversation I had with his potential daughter-in-law and he says,

"That makes sense. She has a whole history behind her name. Family ties. That's important to her. She wouldn't wanna give that up. All our surname tells us is where we came from along the slave trade. Which we already knew it was English/Dutch. Ours means nothing to us. So, it's nothing to give up. Makes sense to take hers."

My initial thought should be "Wow, how progressive of my father to not be tied down to such a patriarchal trope in marriage and be understanding. However, I actually say, "Oh my god, I am your son! Can you just pretend to be on my side for once?! Just pretend! I already know you believe she can do no wrong whatsoever. I know the bias is there for her, but my god does it have to be this blatant?! After all these years now you wanna be all cool and understanding?! Now? This guy."

And I know he's right. I get it. Fine. I'm just saying, damn, give me some favoritism. This one time, she and I walked my Dad back to his car, and she was dead focused on getting a hug from him as she had each encounter. She goes for it and my Dad's all surprised and laughing like, "Oh, hahaa. Okay," and then he looks at me and I'm looking at him for a split second thinking, "oh, is he going to invite me in for a hug next?"

I was about to motion my arms for one and my man goes, "Okay Omar. . . . See you (the fuck) later," then dips into his car and drives off. She does poetry too and she and I had a joke about who would win in a slam and my dad took her side! Again, I am your son! The betrayal!

I sigh my mother's sigh, and I tell my love what he said. She declares, "And that's why George is everybody's favorite Holmon." I never believed in this lifetime, I'd be hearing this, but here we are.

Ironically, one meaning of Holmon is, "Dweller in a hollow" Although she and I will end and not marry, I know three things:

One, the universe will provide her with everything and everyone she deserves (and she deserves the most).

Two, "Everyone wanna be a feminist but don't nobody wanna be a feminist."

And Three, I was my namesake for so long after Mom died. I dwelled in so much empty. She didn't have to pull me out from all that hollow, but she did, each time, and still does whenever I hear her name.

After's After Party

Life
a house party

Karma
a dj

with highlights of your life
reincarnated on vinyl

Death
a downstairs neighbor
always knocking

Death
the one that sneaks into the house party

Death
that moment you notice family and friends
you swore were still here
partying

gone

moved on to an after party
that you don't have an in with yet

Echo of an Epilogue

When you were here, you'd say,
"I won't always be around to do this for you"
When you weren't around anymore you said,

. . .

Isabelle had three children
I'm the youngest
When I was in trouble, she'd stumble through the first
two's names
before getting to mine,

"Kece, Travis, ... Omar"

Depending on how much trouble I was in,
it was my job to just know who she was addressing
"Trav-, Kec——, you know who you are! Come here"

You know how you hear the ocean when you put your
ear to a seashell,
but you know it's not the ocean,
it's just the coincidence that the calm of nothing
sounds so similar

I wish there was something of yours left
that I could put my ear to
and hear the familiar of your voice
stumbling for my name

Proffer

In Track, when running a relay event
the best way to receive a baton pass
is to judge the

distance

of the incoming teammate.
When they're close enough,
The receiver will turn away and sprint forward

The passer may shout an audible call
such as,

"Up!" or "Here! Here! Here!"
to let receiver know they're within passing range.

The receiver will then throw an arm back,
outstretched and high,
palm underhand facing the passer

When the receiver feels the baton within their grasp,
They will grip the baton and pull it into the stride
The passer will let go of the baton
slightly before the receiver's pull

This must all be done within the relay zone
marked by a row of yellow triangles on the track

20 meters apart

If the pass is not received within the zone
the team is disqualified
If the baton is dropped at any point
the team is disqualified
This event is where the idiom
"to pass the baton" stems from,
Meaning, to pass the job or responsibility onto someone

It is a gesture that's more crucial than simple
It depends on both teammates,
like marriage

My sister told me of a time when she saw my father,
Who was then her stepfather
And Mom, who was our mother,
exchanging pet names with one another in the kitchen,
fondness grandfather-clocking between the two,
back and forth

I only know time from when their pendulum stopped,
and all I ever saw them exchange was distance

When I was in Track & Field,
I did the 4x400 metres relay
I always ran final position of the relay team,
the anchor leg

The anchor leg is responsible
for either making up lost ground on the race-leader or
preserving the lead
I never had to make up for lost ground

A few weeks after the funeral,
my father calls,
asks if I've enrolled in something about a 401k
already knowing I haven't

He's frustrated but I think not really at me,
so I ask, "Why are you so adamant about this?"

"Because I want to go to sleep and your mother won't let
me. She keeps coming in my dreams. Telling me to
make sure you're alright. I just wanna get some sleep"

I give the old man some clarity by reminding him
that he and Mom hated talking to each other
I assure him, it's just in his head

Dad says,
"We'd still called each other back and forth.
Each time we did, we talked about you"

When we hang up, I do what my father asks of me,
then imagine Mom,
visiting Dad that night
for the last time,

back in that same kitchen,

walking 20 meters towards him,
casually tossing the baton
while saying,

"Here, your turn."

Precious Little Life

I'm fifteen at a small circus.
My mother is trying to convince me
to ride the elephant.
I don't want to ride the elephant.

I am now on the elephant.

Correction, I am now on the elephant
with a bunch of five-year-olds.

Elephants are self-aware
and able to recognize their own reflections in a mirror.

I'm twenty-one, and Mom is telling me
a story about an elephant in the zoo
that recognized a man that wronged them years ago.

When the man gets close to the cage
the elephant grabs him and chokes him
to death with their trunk.

Mom says,
I wonder what the man did
to piss the elephant off that much.

This prompts me to speak for the elephant and say,

"Mutha fucka I told you I wanted Jif peanut butter!
You thought I couldn't tell that was Skippy?
You thought I wouldn't remember that shit?!"

Mom laughs till her cheeks are all waterfall.

Elephants have the largest brains of all land animals.
The larger the mass, the better the memory.

I am twenty-five
when my mother says she knows
how much I've always wanted a pet,

so she got me one.

I'm like "Oh shit a puppy?" She says,
"Oh. Well you're goin' be disappointed
but it does begin with a p."

In my room there's a bamboo plant
placed inside the back of a ceramic green elephant.

The elephant is posed in mid-march.
She says, "It made me think of you,
how you're always on the go."

I name the elephant after my favorite book.
"Precious Little Life."

I am twenty-six
and writing a poem about the different names
given to describe a group of animals.

My teammate points out that
a group of elephants is called a memory.

Elephants have been known to die
and remain

Standing,
well after death.

I am twenty-six
and Mom is lying down in a hospital bed.

Elephants will travel to where members of their herd
have died and mourn their loss.
I am twenty-six,
and migrating to the hospital for two weeks,
naïve to the inevitable.

I've just turned twenty-seven
and the loss of my mother
has become the elephant in the room.

Migration becomes second nature to me now.

      I move out of our apartment,

I move in with a friend,

        I can move everything but

on.

Weeks later, the friend apologizes for his cat
knocking over my bamboo plant.
He glues the elephant back together,
but the damage is still visible.

How fitting that, if you look close enough
you can see all the cracks in my precious little life.

Anatomy Of A Prayer

1

I can count the number of times I've prayed
on one hand

2

My best friend asks me,
"Why is it every girl you date wants to find God after
they have sex with you?"

I reply,
"I don't know.
Why is it you tell time by saying,
'It's a quarter to whiskey or half past tequila?'"

3

I believe in Murphy's Law:
"Anything that can go wrong,
will go wrong"

4

My father
is a man of science.
I don't know what he believes in.

I'd sooner question if he's found proof to what color
human God bleeds
than ask him

5

My mother is shotgun subtle
when it comes to bad news,
"I rented Erin Brockovich . . .
Julia Roberts has HUUUGE teeth

"By the way the cancer is back.
It's in my liver and spine. . . .
Seriously, her teeth are huge."

She believes in God the way I think that everything will
be okay, but I've been watching her
lose faith in her human,
as the presence of a cane becomes a reminder
that her shotgun subtle is becoming sandcastle,

and, whenever people say she is in their prayers,
I become more of my father's son

trying to configure a formula
for the measurement of prayers,
as if I could calculate how many more it will be
until she is allowed to take sitting up
for granted again.

How many more till I believe everything will be okay

6

I ask her if she is afraid
She says no

I ask her if she thinks this is it
She doesn't know.

Then I ask, "Soooo, between you and me . . .
Do you want my brother to be the one to pull the plug
because he is the least favorite?
Cause I figure, if it's gotta be one of the kids to do it . . .
it might as well be "*that one*".

She laughs,
says my humor always came like a prayer being
answered for her.

7

All along laughter
has been the anatomy of my prayer.

8

My mother
is too stubborn to die.
Her pride is a Scientific Law that states:
"The will to live is not privilege or birthright; it is fight"

In other words,
"I've had two ex-husbands;
if I can survive their bullshit then I can handle this"

I'm running out of life, not running out of fight.

9

Welcome to the rematch three years in the making
introducing the challenger
with a record of 5.8 million knockouts
due to cancer alone.

The white light at the end of the tunnel!
And our champion,
weighing in at
"none of your damn business,"
sporting a record of 15,000 ass whoopings
over a span of three kids

Isabelle "I'll give you something to cry about" Holmon

10

I believe in Murphy's Law,
"Everything that can go wrong
will go wrong."

But I also believe in anomalies,
that everything that can go wrong

will get better.

I believe

the color human that God bleeds is compassion;

and I believe

the will to live is not privilege or birthright.

It is fight,
it is instinct,

Mom, I still believe
that everything

will be okay.

It has been so long, Mom,
since I've said your name out loud

and believed that everything . . .

That everything

would be okay.

ACKNOWLEDGEMENTS

Lupe Fiasco's "The Emperor's soundtrack" plays in the background

I got a lot of people to thank and not that much space to do it in. First and foremost, the entire reason I write and perform is due to Toney Jackson (aka Zach Lost) performing at my high school assembly and saying, "I'm coming back from tomorrow to see how far you've come today." That line is what made me want to do this and is still my North Star.

My teachers, Mr. (Chris) Ryan.
Professor Susan Miller.
Professor Wesley Brown.

A1 educators that are funnier and cooler than fuck.
Pay teachers more than what the fuck they are due.

To folks who kept bothering me to be more or better,
Thank you: Natasha Singh-Holmon, Cristin O'Keefe Aptowicz, William H. Evans, Michael "Big Mike" Bertram, Nicole Homer, Jordan Calhoun, Sarah Kay,

Mahogany Browne, Jive Poetic, Devon Bertram, Eboni Hogan, Falu, Nokuthula, Mackenzie, Elvis, Brie, Rock Lee, everyone at Black Nerd Problems, and every Chace Morris track I kept on repeat during this process.

For those no longer with us:
my mother, Isabelle Holmon,
my uncle, Robert Williams,
my uncle, Wilbert Williams.

For those still here: my sister, Kece,
my brothers, Travis, and George IV,
my father, George Holmon III.

And last but never least,
Isabelle's favorite, her "Little Prince,"
and who this entire collection of poems is for:
my nephew, Damien Noah Fernando.

ABOUT THE AUTHOR

Omar Holmon is an Alumus poet of Rutgers University and has competed in slam poetry for numerous years, with two Final Stage appearances at the National Poetry Slam. He has been featured on Button Poetry, TEDx, a Laphroaig whiskey.

In 2014, Omar Holmon co-founded the Black Nerd Problems website with William Evans, where he spends his days writing essays on pop culture, blackness, and making top quality gifs.

OTHER BOOKS BY BUTTON POETRY

If you enjoyed this book, please consider checking out some of our others, below. Readers like you allow us to keep broadcasting and publishing. Thank you!

Neil Hilborn, *Our Numbered Days*
Hanif Abdurraqib, *The Crown Ain't Worth Much*
Olivia Gatwood, *New American Best Friend*
Donte Collins, *Autopsy*
Melissa Lozada-Oliva, *peluda*
Sabrina Benaim, *Depression & Other Magic Tricks*
William Evans, *Still Can't Do My Daughter's Hair*
Rudy Francisco, *Helium*
Guante, *A Love Song, A Death Rattle, A Battle Cry*
Rachel Wiley, *Nothing Is Okay*
Neil Hilborn, *The Future*
Phil Kaye, *Date & Time*
Andrea Gibson, *Lord of the Butterflies*
Blythe Baird, *If My Body Could Speak*
Desireé Dallagiacomo, *SINK*
Dave Harris, *Patricide*
Michael Lee, *The Only Worlds We Know*
Raych Jackson, *Even the Saints Audition*
Brenna Twohy, *Swallowtail*
Porsha Olayiwola, *i shimmer sometimes, too*
Jared Singer, *Forgive Yourself These
Tiny Acts of Self-Destruction*
Adam Falkner, *The Willies*
Kerrin McCadden, *Keep This To Yourself*
George Abraham, *BIRTHRIGHT*

Available at buttonpoetry.com/shop and more!